MW01104827

Essential Que

How can you use what you know
to help others?

Every Picture
Tells a Story

by Iris Franks
illustrated by Vicki Bradley

Chapter 1
My Sketchbook

My name is Lila. I used to live in a village. I knew everybody. People **greeted** me as I walked to school.

Now I live in America. I live in a big city. I ride the bus to school.

Each day, I look at my sketchbook. I drew pictures of the village where I lived.

There are pictures of my grandmother.
I like the picture of her at the market.
She is buying cacao beans. She makes hot
chocolate with them.

I have a thermos of hot chocolate
in my bag. Mama made it with my
grandmother's cacao paste. One of my
grandmother's **talents** is making chocolate.

My school in America is big. I don't know many people. I have met Martin and Lucia. I have met the twins Dario and Cruz. We wait at the bus stop together. Sometimes I see them playing at the park.

I drew pictures to help me learn their names. I drew Martin and Lucia.

I drew Dario and Cruz. Their family came from Mexico City two years ago. My family came here two months ago.

Martin, Lucia, Dario, and Cruz speak Spanish and English. I speak some Spanish. I speak a little English. My family speaks the **language** of our people. We come from Oaxaca in Mexico.

STOP AND CHECK

Why did Lila draw pictures of her friends?

Chapter 2
The Class Report

Lucia and Martin are talking before school. I can only understand some of the words. They don't **notice** that they have an **audience**.

Lucia keeps saying the words "chocolate" and "cacao." She looks worried. Martin reads from a book about chocolate. Lucia takes notes.

Lucia has to give a report in class this week. I think her report is about chocolate. I want to ask her if I can help. But I am **embarrassed**. I don't have **confidence** in my English.

Then I have an idea. I can use my pictures to tell Lucia about chocolate!

I open my sketchbook.

STOP AND CHECK

How will the sketchbook help Lila?

Before I left Mexico, I drew some pictures of Grandmother. She was making chocolate from cacao beans.

"Lila, you will learn new things in America," said Grandmother. "I want to teach you an old skill."

That day, Grandmother showed me how to make chocolate from cacao beans. I drew a picture for each step.

STOP AND CHECK

How can Lila help Lucia?

Chapter 3
Making Chocolate

I see Lucia at lunch. I feel **shy**, but I go over to her.

"I know how to make chocolate," I say.

"I'm doing a report on chocolate!" says Lucia. "Can you help me, please?"

I show Lucia my pictures.

I show Lucia how my grandmother **roasted** cacao beans over a fire.

The next picture shows how Grandmother rubbed the beans. This helped peel off the skin.

The next picture shows my grandmother
grinding the cacao into a powder. Lucia
asks about the grinding table. I tell her
it is a stone. There is a flame under the
stone. The heat from the flame softens
the cacao powder so it becomes less hard.
Then my grandmother would add sugar
and spices to make a paste.

In the next picture, Grandmother is stirring the chocolate paste into hot water. She uses a wooden whisk.

In the last picture, my grandmother is giving me a cup of hot chocolate.

Then I take out my thermos. I pour
Lucia some hot chocolate.

"This is my grandmother's chocolate,"
I say.

"Thanks! This is delicious," says Lucia,
as she drinks it.

Lucia gives her report a few days later.

"This is a story about the best hot chocolate ever," she says.

At the end, Lucia says, "I want to thank my friend Lila. She helped me with this report."

The teacher shows the class my pictures. I am embarrassed by the **attention**. But I **realize** that I have made a friend.

STOP AND CHECK

What is in Lila's thermos?

Respond to Reading

Summarize

Summarize *Every Picture Tells a Story*. Use details from the story. Your chart may help you.

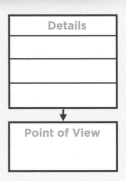

Details

↓

Point of View

Text Evidence

1. What does Lila think about her grandmother? Use an example from the story. Point of View

2. What does the word *softens* on page 12 mean? What clues help you figure it out? Vocabulary

3. Write about how the author shows Lila's point of view in the beginning of the story. Write About Reading

Compare Texts
Read about how Lila and her friends help a neighbor.

Hidden Treasure

One day, Lila was playing ball with Dario and Cruz in their yard. Cruz kicked the ball. It went over the neighbor's fence, so Lila went to get it. She knocked on the neighbor's door.

Mrs. Perez opened the door. "Have you lost your ball? It will be hard to find. The yard is full of weeds," she said.

"We'll clean up your yard then," said Lila.

Illustration: Vicki Bradley

17

The next day, Martin and Lucia went with Lila, Dario, and Cruz to Mrs. Perez's house.

Martin knew a lot about plants.

Mrs. Perez said to Lila, "That's a weed. Please, pull it out," she said.

Martin came over and looked at the plant. "That's not a weed. It's a hollyhock."

"It's a weed," said Mrs. Perez. "Pull it out, Lila."

"That will be a beautiful plant," said Martin. "Don't pull it out."

Mrs. Perez shrugged and walked away.

Some time later, Mrs. Perez thanked Lila for cleaning up her yard.

"What an **achievement**," Mrs. Perez said. "Remember that weed that Martin told us not to pull out?"

"Yes," said Lila.

"Please **apologize** to Martin. Look at this!"

There, in the garden, were plants with tall spikes covered in flowers. They were hollyhocks! Lila took out her sketchbook and drew them to show the others.

Make Connections

How did Martin use his knowledge of plants to help Mrs. Perez? ESSENTIAL QUESTION

How was Lila's talent for drawing useful? Use examples from *Every Picture Tells a Story* and *Hidden Treasure* to support your answer. TEXT TO TEXT

Focus on
Genre

Realistic Fiction Realistic fiction stories are often set in the present. The characters are realistic. That means that they are like real people.

Read and Find *Every Picture Tells a Story* is set in the present. Lila, her grandmother, Martin, and Lucia are realistic characters. What events in the story are things that could happen in real life?

Your Turn

Think of a problem that you have faced. Think of a skill that you have. Tell a friend a story about solving the problem as if you are the main character.